Fearlessly Faithless to Faithfully Fearless

Kyla M. Neil, MTS, BS

Jane,
always remember
that fear has no
place in your life!
Faith over fear

Love,
Sheyla

Devotional Introduction

Faith - the route through which transformation is made; healing is received, power is given, and victory is achieved. There is absolutely nothing we can gain without faith. We can't please God without it, nor can we enter in heaven without it. Yet, so often, we allow fear to take a front-row seat in our lives, robbing us of the rich blessings only faith in God can offer us. Fear is not even a spirit we were designed to have; yet, we invite it into our lives, making it our friend rather than seeing it as the enemy. After all, it's the enemy – Satan - who plants those seeds of doubt that turn into trees of doom and gloom. It's time to stop allowing fear from situations that arise, short or long term, to keep you weak and wimpy. Instead, let your faith allow you to seek God so He can change you into the HEALTHY, PREVAILING, CONQUEROR you are to be.

Day 1

Getting Renewed

Faith Builder

Isaiah 40:28-31

Faith is something every believer must have to survive on this spiritual journey. Not only should you possess it, but it should possess you. It seems simple enough; however, you and I know that living life is not always an easy thing to do. At times, things come along that cause you to be blind-sighted, causing you to stumble and fall, and make you feel like you just won't make it. You get down-right tired. In those moments of weariness, you can find hope in the fact that the Lord can give you fresh strength so that you can continue on the journey. All you need to do is wait on Him. While waiting can also be a challenge, you will realize that the results of waiting - renewed strength and energy, can lead to a harvest of blessings. (Gal. 6:9)

Faith Challenge

What will you do to ensure that you do not become weary in your faith?

_____

_____

_____

_____

_____

_____

_____

_____

_____

_____

_____

_____

_____

_____

Day 2

Act Like You Know

Do your actions reveal the amount of faith you have? When things come up in your life, do you become restless and fearful, losing sleep? Or do you remain joyful and full of peace? Faith is more than just believing God can do all things, but it is also acting as though you know He can. When your finances aren't the best, or your marriage is on shaky ground, or your children aren't behaving the way you want, how will you act? Even if you've received news of a life-threatening illness, how will you act? Becoming worried and fearful are actions that reveal that you don't think God can handle the situation. Praise as opposed to fear should always be our response to the circumstance we encounter in life. Unfortunately, the latter is always the first reaction. Faith causes us to respond where fear will cause us to react. We serve a God who, no matter what takes place in our lives, is more than capable of making sure the outcome works to our advantage and His glory. Remain at peace when life begins to hurl stuff your way, and let your actions say, "Why should I worry, my God can do exceedingly abundantly above all that I ask or think?"

Faith Challenge

What will you do to ensure that your actions reveal unwavering faith?

_____

_____

_____

_____

_____

_____

_____

_____

_____

_____

_____

_____

_____

Day 3

Hope Beyond the Clouds

Faith Builder

Psalm 91

Rain clouds always have a way of making us feel down and gloomy. The inevitable threat of rain tends to make us forget that the sun is still there, even though it's temporarily hidden from us. The clouds eventually give way to sun; however, the gloom has the propensity tampers with our memory. The issues of life bring on the same "doom and gloom" effect on us. Just as rain clouds hide the blue skies and rays of sunlight, so do rough circumstances and situations, when they show up. They hide, or put an overcast of doubt, fear, anxiety, worry, and stress, on the joy the Lord intended us to have in Him. However, the Lord's powerful presence can overshadow the rain clouds of life. It can outshine all of those negative emotions that drift into our lives. We just have to learn to look to Him, past the lingering, doom-filled clouds. David says He was able to find safety just being in God's shadow. God's presence is so powerful that His mere shadow can brighten our gloomiest moments. When we put our faith and trust in God, we will make it through any storm. Just as we know the rain clouds, even after tumultuous storms, eventually give way to sunny blue skies, so will hope in the Lord bring joy, peace, and happiness to our lives. Don't be afraid to look past the clouds. Great things lie beyond them!

Faith Challenge

What will you do to keep the clouds of life from darkening the
path of your spiritual journey?

_____

_____

_____

_____

_____

_____

_____

_____

_____

_____

_____

_____

_____

Day 4

Faith Builder
James 1:2-4

Positive Test Results

What do you dislike most about taking tests? Is it the studying that is needed to make sure you're prepared or the anxiety that fills you before the test? Maybe it's the "waiting for the results" you don't like." Either way, whether we like them or not, tests are needed to know if the proper skills or knowledge have been acquired in a particular area. To find the root cause of a medical issue, tests need to be taken. In order to know if you are qualified for a particular job, a test is given. As believers, tests come our way, not to frustrate us, although they sometimes do. The purpose of tests is so the Lord can develop, strengthen, challenge, and design us for the work that needs to be done for His kingdom. James 1:2-4 says, *"Dear brothers and sisters, when troubles come your way, consider it an opportunity for great joy. For you know that when your faith is tested, your endurance has a chance to grow. So let it grow, for when your endurance is fully developed, you will be perfect and complete, needing nothing."* (NLT). So, the next time you encounter a test in your faith walk, don't become fearful. Your job is to make sure your test scores speak highly of the One who prepared you for the test!

Faith Challenge

What can you do to ensure you don't get test anxiety during your next test?

_____

_____

_____

_____

_____

_____

_____

_____

_____

_____

Day 5

Faith that Pleases

Do you know that it is possible to walk this Christian journey without faith? It's not wise to make the journey without it, but it is certainly possible. There are setbacks, however, to having a faithless walk. For instance, missing out on blessings intended for us due to a lack of faith. Hebrews 11 speaks of the blessings that came to those who walked in faith. Abraham and Sarah, after waiting 15 years, were blessed with their promised son, Isaac. Then, Rahab, who hid the two spies, was blessed to be in the lineage of Christ. Although these three persons did not experience the full extent of God's promises, they continued to wait in faith, based on what they did experience. Having faith in God pleases Him, but it also makes it possible to obtain the unseen things the Lord has willed for your life and those who come after you. Most of all, it gives you access to the One who can offer you a life of pure joy, complete happiness – eternal bliss. A lack of faith causes you to constantly live in fear of the unknown instead of being filled with hope of what's to come. Don't be foolish enough to walk this journey and end up with nothing to show for it.

Faith Challenge

What will you do to make sure you have God-pleasing faith?

_____

_____

_____

_____

_____

_____

_____

_____

_____

_____

_____

Day 6

Faith Builder

**Handing Over Control**

Mark 9:14-24

Control: The power to influence or direct people or the course of events. Whether we are willing to admit it or not, we all want to be in control. It can be with but certainly not limited to our jobs, our mates/significant others, family, friends, and/or the various situations that arise in our lives. For example, as parents we want to control our children by dictating where they go, the type of friends they keep, the type of activities in which they are involved, and so forth. It is the fear of a negative or painful outcome that causes us to try to control situations. However, the detriment of doing so is that we hinder the work God wants to do for growth to occur. Some things have to happen in order for God's development process to take place. It's difficult to step out of the way and let life happen to your child, or even yourself. You hope for the best but are not able to guarantee it. In Mark, we read about a father who struggled with believing for the best outcome for His son. The father tried to handle it but nothing worked. It wasn't until after he brought his son before the Lord that healing took place. Instead of us trying to control our loved ones or situations, let us take them before the Lord, even in the uncertainties. Relinquish control, step away and watch how He perfectly handles things.

Faith Challenge

What will you do to ensure you are not trying to control God's plans for your life?

_____

_____

_____

_____

_____

_____

_____

_____

_____

Day 7

The Pleasure Stealer

Faith Builder
John 10:7-10

Several years ago, during a visit with my rheumatologist, she mentioned how impressed she was with my MRI's. I thought it was a compliment until she said, "I don't even know how you're walking, with all the arthritis!" We just laughed. I was just determined not to allow the pain to keep me from living a productive and joyful life. Imagine if we learned to have the same mindset when dealing with the painful moments we encounter on our faith journey. Instead of handing things over to the Lord, we try to work through things our way, which only brings on unnecessary stress and worry. We allow our pain to rob us of the very thing Christ died for us to have. The Lord did not intend for us to live lives filled with pain and misery. John 10 tells us the Lord says, "…I have come that they may have life, and that they may have it more abundantly." The abundance of which He speaks is not material but spiritual - joy and peace. To receive the wealth of joy the Lord desires us to have, we must learn to let go of the things that tend to rob us of the joy He died for us to have.

Faith Challenge

What will you do to make sure you don't allow painful times to be a killjoy in your life and to your witness?

_____

_____

_____

_____

_____

_____

_____

_____

_____

Day 8

Light in Your Darkness

Faith Builder

1 Thessalonians 5: 4-5

Have you ever had to move about your house amid a power failure? I'm sure it wasn't too difficult since your home is a place of familiarity to you. However, have you ever had to do it in a place where you weren't as familiar? It isn't easy maneuvering in the dark in an unfamiliar place. It causes a sense of uneasiness, and not knowing which way to go can sometimes cause pure fear. When operating out of total and complete faith, we can experience those same emotions. Sometimes we will find ourselves in a complete state of darkness, meaning we have absolutely no idea of how a particular situation is going to turn out, and the only thing we can do is trust God. Usually, the hardest part of trusting is accepting God's will, especially if your heart's desire may or may not be His will for you. Paul tells us that we should never be caught off guard by the dark since we are children of light – Christ. When we encounter those dark places in our lives, we have to be willing to have enough faith and trust in God, regardless of how dark, hard, painful, and fearful it may become. The Lord is going to work it out for our good and ultimately, His glory. He is the light in our darkness. We can be assured that even the darkest of times won't overshadow His power to shine victoriously in our lives.

Faith Challenge

What will you do to ensure that your dark times don't outshine
your bright future?

_____

_____

_____

_____

_____

_____

_____

_____

_____

_____

Day 9

The Power of One Word

ANXIETY: a feeling of worry, nervousness, or unease, typically about an imminent event or something with an uncertain outcome. WORRY: give way to anxiety or unease; allow one's mind to dwell on difficulty or troubles. FEAR: an unpleasant emotion caused by the belief that someone or something is dangerous, likely to cause pain, or a threat. Many times, these three words drive us more than we ought to allow them, and they tend to dictate how we handle most of life's issues. Fortunately for us, as believers, there is only one word that counteracts them, and it is God's Word. In God's Word, your response to ANXIETY is in Phil. 4:6-7. If you go to Matthew 6:25-34, you will find what should be your reaction to worry. Then, if you're looking for a solution to stop being fearful, you could go to II Timothy 1:7. While we have many words to describe many things, believers only need one word to help us as we encounter the issues of life. It is the word FAITH, upon which God's Word is centered. This single word sums up all we need to have to live a life free of anxiety, worry, and fear. Remember, it isn't always about quantity but rather the quality that makes the difference.

Faith Challenge

What will you do to ensure that God's Word, and not your
emotions are the driving force in your life?

_____

_____

_____

_____

_____

_____

_____

_____

_____

Day 10

Waiting for Instructions

Faith Builder

2 Chronicles 20:15-17

"You will not need to fight in this battle. Position yourselves, stand still and see the salvation of the LORD, who is with you, O Judah and Jerusalem! Do not fear or be dismayed; tomorrow go out against them, for the LORD is with you." In this passage, Jahaziel is encouraging King Jehoshaphat and the people of Judah and Jerusalem to stand, without fear, amidst a pending battle. There was absolutely nothing they needed to do because they had already been given instructions. The instructions were simply to stand still and see. It's amazing how we can take the simplest of instructions and complicate them by interfering in God's business. We try to take control of a situation that was never ours in the first place. Then, when things get messed up, we go to God upset saying, "Lord, I don't understand. What went wrong?" Fear will cause us to hinder God's perfectly planned outcome because of our poorly manipulated schemes. Standing still and watching how the Lord is going to work out our situations is not an easy thing to do, and so we cannot try to do it through our strength, just as Jehoshaphat couldn't win the battle on his own. Our only responsibility is to pray in faith, wait for the instructions, and follow them when given. Don't be concerned about how long it takes for an answer, just know God will. He didn't fail the Israelites, and He won't fail you.

Faith Challenge

What will you do to make certain your impatience doesn't obstruct God's instructions for your life?

_____

_____

_____

_____

_____

_____

_____

_____

_____

_____

Day 11

Sudden Changes

Faith Builder

Deuteronomy 31:6-8

In June 2013, I had the opportunity to attend the National Baptist Congress of Christian Education Annual Session in St. Louis, MO. I was a bit nervous because it was only my second time flying. I remember, at one point in the flight looking out the window and seeing sunny, blue skies. I looked away for a split second, and when I looked again, we were in the midst of the clouds. I became fearful because I could no longer see anything around me. How often is it that we operate the same way in our faith? As long as things are going well, we're fine. But the moment "storm clouds" come and we can't see ahead: we get out of sorts and fear sets in. The same reminder the Lord gave to the Israelites in Deuteronomy 31 holds true for you today. There is no need for you to be fearful because He is always with you. As a matter of fact, fear is not even a spirit we've been given according to 2 Tim. 1:7. We must be ever careful not to give fear the control over us that we so often do. Be encouraged in knowing that, although things change in the blink of an eye, God is in control. He is ready and more than capable of handling anything that comes up in our lives, whether it's by way of our hand or His.

Faith Challenge

What will you do to make sure sudden changes don't keep you
from seeing clearly?

_____

_____

_____

_____

_____

_____

_____

_____

_____

_____

_____

Day 12

Take Rest in the Storm

Faith Builder

Matthew 8: 23-27

What is the depth of your insight?? Can you look at a painting and see the artist's soul, not just the colors of paint? Can you see past that unruly child to the greatness he/she is destined to become? Can you see past your problems to the lesson that is to be learned? That was the problem with the disciples in Mark 6:47-51. Their eyes only saw the fierce storm winds and turbulent waves. They weren't even able to recognize Jesus when He showed up amid the storm. The amazing part was that they were with Him EVERY DAY, witnessing His miraculous power firsthand. How can you be around the Lord and still not know Him? We are very much like the disciples. We say we know who Jesus is; however, when life gets the best of us, we quickly forget and find it hard to recognize His face or even His past victories in our life. If we allow our heart and spirit to "see" what our eyes see, as we walk with the Lord, I guarantee it will not be hard to recognize Him when He shows up. Are you willing to look deeper, and even beyond when the waves of life's storms look like they may overpower you?

Faith Challenge

What will you do to make sure you remain at rest when life is
tossing you around?

_____

_____

_____

_____

_____

_____

_____

_____

_____

_____

Day 13

Be Still for a Moment

Faith Builder

Psalm 46:10

Isaiah 30:15

There is nothing like a little peace and quiet in your life. Time to get away from the noise of life. However, for some, being still makes them feel as though they're unproductive. Yet, for others, a strong fear comes when they have to spend time alone. The quietness takes them to an unwanted place of remembering painful times in their lives. Fear of being still and quiet can cause us to miss the benefits that come from having moments of quietness. In one of today's passages, God gives the instruction to "Let be and be still, and know (recognize and understand) that I am God" (AMP). In our second passage, God promises that "In quietness and in [trusting] confidence shall be your strength." In both passages, God assures us there is no reason to fear being still. Fear of being unproductive can cause you to run yourself so much you become ineffective, which is just a bad as being unproductive. And fear of spending time alone, because of the voices from your past you don't want to hear, will cause you to miss hearing the one voice that can drown out all the others. Take some time today to get still and be quiet and meet up with the Lord. He's waiting to give you what you need.

Faith Challenge

What will you do to guarantee you have consistent times of quiet
and make the most out of those times?

_____

_____

_____

_____

_____

_____

_____

_____

_____

_____

_____

Day 14

Risk Takers for Christ

Faith Builder

Philippians 1: 6-14

During one of my classes in seminary, the professor posed the question, "What is it that keeps you from responding to what God is doing in the world, and what do you risk in responding? My two-fold answer held a single theme – fear. Fear of responsibility and of the unknown. The unknown factor meant that I would have to be willing to take the risk to find out what God wanted me to do for Him. How many of us find ourselves fearing the unknown? Then, allow that fear to purposely cause us to limit ourselves in doing the work of the Lord. The key thing to remember is that fear has absolutely no impact on the plans the Lord has willed for our lives. It will not prevent what is meant to be. Today's scripture passage makes that very clear. The Lord has willed great things in all of us when it comes to doing His work. It is imperative that we remember that, no matter how much we may try to stifle it, God's work will be carried out. We have no reason to be fearful of what the Lord has placed in us nor of what He wants us to do. We must also remember that we are not alone in this journey (Heb. 13:5); even though it may be scary not knowing what is to come. Jesus wasn't afraid to give His life for us, so we must not be afraid to risk giving ours for Him. We have so much to gain if we do.

Faith Challenge

What are you willing to risk to make sure your part in God's Kingdom work is not left undone?

_____

_____

_____

_____

_____

_____

_____

_____

_____

_____

Day 15

Keep Your Focus

Faith Builder

Matthew 14:23-33

Global Positioning Systems (GPS) are a great resource to use when traveling. They help us get to our exact location. All we have to do is listen to the voice that's guiding us. The other option, instead of using the voice as a guide, is to simply look at the system to find out our next move. However, there is one thing you have to be mindful of - do not have your eyes off the road too long. Taking your eyes off the road one second too long could lead to a detrimental outcome. I am reminded of when Peter attempted to walk on water. As long as Peter kept His eyes on Christ as He spoke, he was fine. However, the moment his focus shifted from the Master to the stormy waves and darkness, he became scared and began to sink. All Peter had to do was keep looking at Jesus and listen to His voice to be properly directed. Just as the voice in the GPS guides us, so will the Holy Spirit do with us. On this spiritual journey, we must always remember to keep our eyes focused on the Lord; the One who is always in control, no matter how turbulent the storms of life may become. Our sight and hearing are connected to one another, and if Christ is our main focus, we can be sure He will keep us on the right path (Rom 10:17).

Faith Challenge

What will you do to maintain the proper focus on your
faith walk?

_____

_____

_____

_____

_____

_____

_____

_____

_____

_____

_____

Day 16

All: Are you willing to give it?

All: the whole of one's possession, resources, or energy (Merriam-Webster). Given that explanation, how many of us are willing to give all of something? More specifically, our hearts. If you have ever been hurt or disappointed, that can be a difficult task to do. However, what if it is the Lord asking it of us? Does that make any difference? As much as I trust the Lord, a part of me continues to struggle with wholeheartedly trusting Him, and I recognize that it has so much to do with my being let down so many times by people. It is almost as though I am putting God within the same parameters of man, whose very nature, unlike God's, makes failing an inevitability. In Proverbs 3, we are instructed to trust the Lord with all our hearts and to acknowledge Him in all our ways. The Hebrew meaning for all, in this passage, means the whole of; totality. In order for the Lord do what He's willed to do in our lives, we must be willing to give up all our fears, misconceptions, past hurts and manipulative tactics, which prevent Him from taking up full residency in the place that controls us – our hearts, and give Him complete reign over it. The Lord willingly gave up His life so that we could have an amazingly abundant one. It's only fair that we give up our whole heart to show Him His death was not in vain.

Faith Challenge

What will you do to ensure that you trust the Lord with no reservations about His capabilities?

_____

_____

_____

_____

_____

_____

_____

_____

_____

_____

Day 17

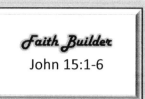

Faith Builder
John 15:1-6

A Clear Connection

Have you ever been on a cordless phone and moved too far from the base? The farther away you get, the more static you hear. And when you get too far, you lose your connection altogether. The same thing happens when we stray too far from our base - the Lord. The base is the source of the power and in order for the receiver to get a strong signal, it has to remain close to the base. When we stop having that personal time with God and coming to fellowship with other believers, our connection weakens, and it makes it hard for us to hear. The static of life's issues clogs our ears and our minds, and we don't handle them as well as we ought. One thing we must recognize is that, just like the phone, the connection is not lost because the base has been moved. It's lost because the receiver has moved from the base. The Lord never moves. It's us, the receiver who moves causing us to become temporarily weak until we get back to the base and reconnect. The Lord already promised that He would never leave us, so we can't blame any inference on Him. In order for us to be productive - bear fruit in our lives, we have to abide in Him. We can't produce anything if we are not properly nourished, and the only way to get it is to be connected to the source.

Faith Challenge

What will you do to make sure you don't move from your source
of power and strength?

_____

_____

_____

_____

_____

_____

_____

_____

_____

_____

_____

Day 18

The Developing Process

Faith Builder

James 1:1-4

Do you remember the old Polaroid cameras? The camera had its own built-in developing system. So, when a picture was taken, it was only a matter of minutes before you were holding it in your hands, admiring it. God has designed His own developing system for us as well, except for one difference. Where Polaroid's film affords us instant results, God's process takes time. And that's where we get ourselves into trouble at times. We want things in our lives to be perfect right away. God, on the other hand, wants to make sure that not only is it perfect but also durable. The writer of James chapter one encourages the believer to have joy during the "fiery" times. It is not that we find joy in the un-pleasantries of life; rather, joy is the result of an anticipated hope of a successful outcome. We just have to press our way through. I encourage all of us not to be so quick and in a hurry to be developed because there's a chance we may mess something up. The one thing about instant film is that when we touch it before it completely dries, it gets smudged, and then you have to take another picture. The only problem is, you may not get the exact pose. Fortunately for us, when we smudge God's work, He's able to make us look even better than the original shot!

Faith Challenge

What will you do to make sure you keep your hands-off God's
development of you?

_____

_____

_____

_____

_____

_____

_____

_____

_____

_____

Day 19

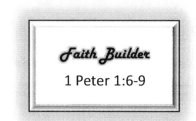

Faith Builder

1 Peter 1:6-9

The Perfect Amount of Heat

Microwaves are one of the most convenient appliances in our kitchen. You can heat up something quickly and then be on your merry way. There's one problem, however, that we've all encountered one time with the microwave. It's when we go to eat our food and find out it wasn't all the way heated. You see, while microwaves are convenient, they are not always thorough. And we end up frustrated because we now have to re-heat the item or discard it because it didn't properly finish the first time. At times, this is how we operate on our faith journey. We encounter situations that will require us to have to wait. But we want to rush and hurry through the process, most likely to avoid the pain associated with waiting. We want everything to happen instantaneously, not always realizing that sometimes we just aren't in the position - mentally, emotionally, physically or spiritually, to handle instant gratification. Peter tells us we're going to have some rough, troubling times. However, we can be encouraged to know that, if we endure, there will be praise that only the heat can bring out. The fire makes sure we're completely finished on the inside so that our outward appearance reveals something of great worth. When we learn to wait on God instead of rushing His process, we won't have to be like that dinner plate needing to be put back in, but with a tad bit more heat.

Faith Challenge

What will you do to make sure you don't have to be reheated too
many times throughout your faith journey?

_____

_____

_____

_____

_____

_____

_____

_____

_____

_____

Day 20

Praise Is What I Do

Faith Builder
Psalm 150

As we travel on the road of faith, it is important for us to realize that praise has to be one of our weapons against the enemy's tactics. So easy is it for us to break down and cry and give in to the pain of our struggles, wallowing in self-pity and walking around with the "woe is me" syndrome. By doing so, we allow the enemy to put us exactly where he wants us to be - defenseless, weak, easily manipulated and controlled. It's time to stop giving him that power and begin using the power that lies within us. When things are going wrong with your children… PRAISE HIM. When things are not right in your marriage… PRAISE HIM. When your job is in limbo… PRAISE HIM. When you don't know where your next meal is going to come from… PRAISE HIM. When the pain is just too much to bear… PRAISE HIM. Even when everything is going just right… PRAISE HIM. I encourage you today to not only praise God for the things He has already done, but even more for what He's going to do. Praise Him as you endure whatever it is you're going through so that when you come out, you're already in the right position and posture.

Faith Challenge

What will you do to remain in a perpetual place of praise during challenging times?

_____

_____

_____

_____

_____

_____

_____

_____

_____

_____

Day 21

A Firm Foundation

Faith Builder

Psalm 62

There's this praise song I used to love to sing, and it goes like this; "If you're standing on the solid rock, and you know the power that you've got. Satan cannot prevail, Satan cannot prevail. Praise the Lord, everybody praise the Lord." When we got to the 'Praise the Lord' part, everyone would get up from their seats, waving their hands with joy and excitement. Knowing that, as long as we stand on the word of God, we have the power to overcome any situation that comes up against us. We can look at David and how confident he was in the Lord in the midst of danger. In Ps. 62:2, he says, "He only is my rock and my salvation; He is my defense; I shall not be greatly moved." Verse six says the exact thing with the exception of one word – greatly. The word greatly implies there was an increase in faith that came about as David's confidence in the Lord grew. As we continue to bring our problems to the Lord, our faith grows and causes us to be more victorious over the enemy, and less fearful of him and his tactics. There is no need to become discouraged. You only need to remember the power that you have because of the unsinkable ROCK on which you stand.

Faith Challenge

What will you do to ensure that your faith remains strong when
you're on shaky ground?

_____

_____

_____

_____

_____

_____

_____

_____

_____

_____

Day 22

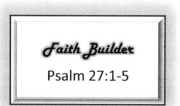

Faith Builder

Psalm 27:1-5

The Calm Life

Have you ever become nervous about something that hasn't even taken place yet? You think about what you will have to do and then your mind sprints ahead of you. You begin to think about the "what ifs", and the "I'm not sure if I can," or even the "maybe this isn't a good idea." We cause ourselves to panic prematurely, thereby giving the enemy room to come in and begin strategically planning his method of attack. The assault weapons he uses are fear, worry, and doubt. Even worse, sometimes we allow those three weapons to wreak havoc even when the Lord clearly tells us, in His Word, that we have nothing to fear. In Psalm 27, David is declaring that he is confident in the Lord's ability to handle any and everything that he will come up against. He was not worried about what was before him nor of what was to come. He remained calm and confident. That should be our response to life's uncertainties as well. You should never be nervous about what life has in store for you. Just pray, relax, and trust God for His planned outcome. Even begin to praise Him in advance for that victory. We need not jump the gun. It only sets us up for failure; something Satan loves to see happen. Keep your mind on Christ and know that God is working everything out for you. In the words of Bobby McFerrin, "Don't worry, be happy."

Faith Challenge

What will you do to make sure your nerves don't make you jump ahead of God?

_____

_____

_____

_____

_____

_____

_____

_____

_____

_____

Day 23

Elevation through Opposition

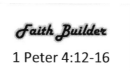

Faith Builder

1 Peter 4:12-16

I am sure you, like most people, dread opposition. On the other hand, however, there are those of us who like being promoted or elevated. While none of us likes opposition, as believers, we must realize that without it, there would be no opportunities for advancement. The Lord permits challenging times to come into our lives, either by His hand, our own, or the hand of the enemy. Yet, without them, there would be no way of building the confidence we need to walk in the power that allows us to prevail over the challenges. Opposition and adversity are needed to give us opportunities to be elevated in Christ, which brings us closer to Him and allows our testimony of who He is and what He'll do to be true and sincere. In fact, Jesus told us to expect opposition if we're going to follow Him. In our passage, Peter says that our adversarial times are nothing more than a spiritual filtering process, which helps remove anything that would hinder us looking like Christ. And while we are told to expect challenges and suffering, we're also told not to be fearful of them. Jesus said, "Be of good cheer" because His death overpowered our troubles (John 16:33). Take heart in knowing that your ability to withstand the struggles and challenges in life will lead you to the greatest level of elevation, which is in glory with the Lord.

Faith Challenge

What will you do to make sure you don't allow opposition to keep you from getting ahead?

_____

_____

_____

_____

_____

_____

_____

_____

_____

_____

Day 24

Sleeping with the Enemy

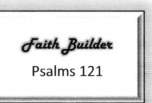

Faith Builder

Psalms 121

Life consumes our minds daily. Thoughts of how things are going to work out are constantly roaming around in our minds, causing us to live in a constant state of manipulation. We are always spending our time figuring out how we are going to make things work in our favor. And all that does is lead to worry. Then, we go to bed, laying our worry on the pillow beside us, allowing it to disrupt what should be a peaceful night's rest. At one point, for me, it was so bad that it was as if I could feel my mind moving a mile a minute, in my sleep. The concept of sleep was nothing more than a figment of my imagination. All because of my dreadful nemesis of a bed partner – **WORRY**. I'm sure many of you are or have been in that same boat. Why is it, though, that we allow worry to disrupt or take away our sleep when we have someone who never "slumbers nor sleeps?" Psalm 121 reminds us there's no need for us to lose sleep when He's there to keep us and handle all our concerns - all the ins and outs of our lives. Stop losing sleep and waking up with bags under your eyes. Besides, the only thing bags are good for is carrying you and your things to a place of clear blue water and white sandy beaches.

Faith Challenge

What will you do to make sure you don't allow worry to consume you?

_____

_____

_____

_____

_____

_____

_____

_____

_____

_____

Day 25

Effective Pain Management

Faith Builder

2 Corinthians 12: 9-10

Managing pain, whether it be physical, emotional or mental, is something millions of people have to deal with daily, and it can be done through a variety of ways. A person suffering from physical pain may manage it through medications or physical therapy. Whereas, someone dealing with mental or emotional pain may treat it by going to a therapist or psychiatrist. Whatever is the cause of the pain, most people just want to find a manageable way to treat it so that it doesn't cause disruption in their daily life activities. As a believer, how do you manage the pains you experience on this faith walk? Pain that comes from experiencing failure, job loss, divorce, loneliness, even death. Often times, we manage by acting as though we're okay by holding it in and masking it with a phony smile and a fake praise, until something or someone comes along to trigger it and we lash out. The most successful and effective way to manage your pain is allow it to weaken you, so that your inner strength – the Holy Spirit, can be activated. Just as medicine targets an internal area to ease the pain, so does the Holy Spirit. He targets your heart, which holds all your pain and your mind, which dictates how you handle it. The Lord never intended for our pain to manage us. He gave us His word, which is the best prescription we could ever use.

Faith Challenge

What will you do to make sure your pain management regime doesn't leave you with negative side effects?

_____

_____

_____

_____

_____

_____

_____

_____

_____

_____

Day 26

Beauty Comes Out of Struggles

Faith Builder

2 Corinthians 4:16-18

Transformation can be a most rewarding process, but it does not come without struggle. I am reminded of a butterfly, and the metamorphic process it goes through to become the beautiful creature we see. Metamorphosis comes from the Greek word, *Metamorphoo* which means transform or change to form. A butterfly, which was once a caterpillar, is changed into a flying adult when it emerges from the cocoon. A key point to remember is that, for the butterfly to be completely transformed, it must go through the process of struggling to break through its cocoon. It is that struggle that ensures its wings are strong enough to carry its body. If the process gets interrupted, the butterfly remains underdeveloped and is not able to complete its life mission – to reproduce. Like the butterfly, we too must endure some struggles, and remain in them until the Lord is confident that we are developed enough to stand strong in Him. Our struggles, which are momentary, are meant to draw us closer to the Lord, and the closer we get to Him, the more we are transformed to look like Him – holy and righteous (Eph. 4:24). When you change the way you view your struggles (Rom. 12:2), you can begin seeing them as the Lord's way of using us to be His models of handiwork to the world.

Faith Challenge

What will you do to make sure you don't allow your struggles to leave you weak and underdeveloped?

_____

_____

_____

_____

_____

_____

_____

_____

_____

_____

Day 27

Embracing Change

Fall is one of the most refreshing and beautiful times of the year. The weather is more comfortable. The leaves change into these gorgeous, vibrant colors. I always look forward to the season of fall and all its wonderful changes. There is another season of change that we experience as well. It is those seasons of change that take place in our lives. The happy seasons. The stormy seasons. The painful seasons. Even the growing seasons. The funny thing about change is that it takes place, whether we are ready for it to take place or not. Three key things to remember about change are: 1) change is inevitable, 2) change is needed, and 3) change is good. God allows change to come into our lives to move us from what we know to be comfortable to what He knows to be our destiny. We need not fear change but rather welcome it, to the point of anticipating it. We need to embrace, with much joy, the pain we experience during our growth spurts. It may seem as if it's easier said than done, and in the beginning it is, but it's also doable because we have Christ (Phil. 4:13). As we pass through each season of life, we grow closer to God, stronger in our walk, and deeper in our faith. I encourage you to look at change not as an enemy but an ally. Think of it like this, how do you expect to see God if you don't want to change? (I Corinthians 15:52)

Faith Challenge

What will you do to make sure your seasonal life changes keep you looking lively and vibrant?

_____

_____

_____

_____

_____

_____

_____

_____

_____

Day 28

Who Will Answer?

Faith Builder

2 Timothy 1: 7-12

Years ago, my mother made a door hang that read, "FEAR KNOCKED AT THE DOOR. FAITH ANSWERED. NO ONE WAS THERE." Can you imagine what must be going through the mind of the person who's knocking at your door as they read it? At some point in our faith journey, we have to begin operating in the faith God instructed us to have. It is the same faith that Paul speaks of in Hebrews 11. The faith our forefathers lived is the same faith that must govern our lives. They did not allow what their eyes saw deter them from the blessings God promised to give them. Even those like Moses and Abraham, who kept hoping even though they never saw the results of their faith. It is time to stop walking around fearing the outcome of our situations – present or future. God has already told us that we have not been given a spirit of fear (2 Timothy 1:7). No longer will fear be our best friend and life travel companion. It is time to begin walking more confidently, knowing that God already knows what He desires to happen in our lives, and that what He has willed for our lives will come to be, through good times and bad times. The next time you hear a knock at your door, let your faith be the one to answer. As a matter of fact, do not even let fear think that answering is an option.

Faith Challenge

What will you do to ensure that your faith is bold enough to answer the challenges of life?

_____

_____

_____

_____

_____

_____

_____

_____

_____

_____

_____

Day 29

Faith-stretching Challenges

Faith Builder

Phil. 3:12-14

Have you ever noticed how rubber bands aren't of much unless they've been stretched a bit? Try using a new one and see just how much you can get it to hold. I guarantee, not too much. It doesn't have quite enough give yet. You have to stretch it out a few times for it to be able to be used the way you want it to be. That's how it works with our faith. There are things the Lord wants us to do for Him, but it isn't until we're stretched, by way of challenges and struggles, that we're able to recognize what is in us. The only way our faith will grow is if it gets stretched, and that involves us having the courage to acknowledge our fears, embrace them, and then face them head-on. The key, however, is recognizing that we have to depend on the Lord, not ourselves. He's already given us the strength we need to succeed through the indwelling power of the Holy Spirit. Always remember, He is strong enough to secure us, even when we feel like we're being stretched too thin. And we can rest assured that He will not let us pop, no matter how tight things get for us.

Faith Challenge

What will you do to make sure your challenges help you continue
to grow in the Lord?

_____

_____

_____

_____

_____

_____

_____

_____

_____

_____

Day 30

Survival of the Fittest

Faith Builder

Isaiah 43:18 -19

Joshua 1:6-9

Do you realize that fear, doubt, and worry are the enemy's most effective assault weapons against the believer? They also make him most successful at getting us to forget about past victories. After all, it has been and continues to be his aim to keep us weary, weak, and warped. But you know what? That's all in the past. Forget about it. Today is a new day. The Lord is doing a new thing in you and me. The enemy's weapons - fear, doubt, worry, along with anxiety, depression, anger, resentment, pain, bitterness, unforgiven - that once overpowered us, we no longer have to allow them to prevail against us. Instead of succumbing to the enemy's lies, I encourage us to follow the Lord's command in Joshua 1, which is to be strong and courageous. However, to do that, we must let go of fear and walk in unwavering faith. I know we may not be able to see what lies ahead, but the Lord can, and that's all that matters. Are you ready to move from fearfully faithless to faithfully fearless? Or has the enemy not quite weakened you to the point of death? Just remember though, only the strong survive!

Faith Challenge

What will you do to ensure that your faith remains strong?

_____

_____

_____

_____

_____

_____

_____

_____

_____

_____

_____

Day 31

The Right Coverage

Faith Builder

Romans 6:1-7

John 11:25

The slogan for Independence Blue Cross is Live Fearless. We know their logo is a bold blue cross. The company's mission is to "inspire a more FEARLESS NATION" by providing health coverage that is not only affordable but also reliable. Many of their commercials are aimed at giving assurance to its millions of members with the statement, "You are protected with the compassion of a cross that's been trusted for over 75 years." The cross referenced here is about protecting and preserving our health. However, there is a more important cross. It is the one that protects us from death. Where Blue cross has been covering people for over 75 years, the cross on Calvary has been covering us for over 2,000 years. Because of that cross, a thief entered glory. Because of that cross, we are able to live in freedom. Most of all, because of that cross, we have eternal life. The cross is a wonderful thing, and now is the time to start walking in the boldness you have because of the cross. Make sure your family and friends do as well. It's important to have the right coverage for your health because anything can happen. But it's even more to make sure we know and live under the coverage of Calvary's cross. It's one thing to live healthily, but it's another thing to be able to live fearlessly, and that's only possible because of the cross.

Faith Challenge

What will you do to make sure there is no lapse in your coverage?

_____

_____

_____

_____

_____

_____

_____

_____

_____

_____

_____

Note of encouragement

You have just completed 31-days of challenging your faith to be bigger than your fears. My prayer for both you (and I) is that these 31-days will not end here. Instead, it will turn into our way of life. The Lord desires the absolute best for us, and the only way to live out that best life is to accept His way of growing our faith, through His Word and our challenges. Once we can get to a place where we anticipate our faith builders, with an attitude of joy, fear will no longer have power over us. We know that fear is nothing more than False Evidence Appearing Real. However, now it is time for us realize that faith is **F**-Fully **A**-Acknowledging **I**-I'm **T**-Truly **H**-His. When we remember to whom it is that we belong, we can face any challenge head-on and not flinch an inch. Faith over fear is the life we want, so let's go out and get what belongs to us.

About the author

Kyla M. Neil is a collaborating author for The Purposed Woman 365 Day Devotional, which made Amazon's Best Seller list for new devotional books. She is currently working on her next book entitled Worth the Push, which she hopes will motivate women to press through the challenges of living with depression and anxiety, to achieve a joyful and productive life. She leads the women's ministry at her church, Jones Memorial Baptist Church, where she mentors women on living fearlessly for the Lord. Kyla has a Bachelor of Science in Behavioral Health Counseling from Drexel University and a Master of Theological Studies from Palmer Theological Seminary. Kyla currently resides in Philadelphia, Pa. with her three adult daughters and one grandson, by whom she is affectionately called Yaya.

Made in the USA
Lexington, KY
16 November 2019

57154135R00039